The Reluctant Poet

Series 2

By Vance Johnson

ISBN 979-8-9865579-9-1

Table of Contents

Acknowledgements

1. Two Bright Stars

2. Love Her

3. Dreaming

4. Life

5. No Key

6. About Happiness

7. Anticipation

8. Serendipity

9. In These Times

10. She Knew

Acknowledgements

Dora Crewshaw (Harrisburg, PA) – Editing

Betti Guerra – Editing and creative inspiration

Tyson Amir (Author of "Black Boy Poems") – The narrative idea for my work came from his creative influence and mentorship.

Ronald A White (Author of "Centurion Justice") Creative influence and mentorship.

Dakota Danna – Creative Influence

Helen Davis - Editing

Narrative for Two Bright Stars

I wrote this poem for a set of identical twins
that had graduated from high school. One Lla
and one Jas.

Two Bright Stars

Two Bright Stars
Shining In the same sky
Two bright stars
Move in different directions.

Each star to glow and grow.
To spread their uniqueness
Further than before.
Two bright stars
To liberate who they are!

One star Jas
Special in her way.
One star Lla
A scholar they say.
Hooray! Hooray! For graduation day

Narrative for Love Her

A generic Valentine

Love Her

From the top of the morning

Moving closer to each other, fawning

Locking eyes of know-ing-ness

Awaiting another day of happiness

A light kiss on the cheek

My heart swells and love I seek

Why I react so completely with you

With just a mere touch from you.

I will never know how this comes to be

I just know love is great for me.

Narrative for Dreaming

This poem speaks to the idea that we should all have "Dreams"!!

Dreaming

To dream is a wonderful gift

    Not the one of nighttime fantasy

But the wide awake lift

    The one we create in our mind and see

Our daily creation by design, plotting

    Devising a foolproof plan

Only you can define how the dream will be

revealed to man.

Narrative for Life

These are words to live by!!

Life

Enjoy the journey!

Be thankful for where you are,

Rejoice over how far you have come

Keep walking one step at a time

With hope and confidence in who you are..

Narrative for "No Key"

A couple I have known for years have
continued to have a loving relationship.

No Key

As you saw me driving by

Love, peace, and happiness on my side,

There was another who knew me far better

This one who crossed the sands with me, my

brother!

Making you my sister!

What a special spirit you have in regards to me!

Like the mountains that surround our city

You and he remain!

How awesome a relationship! One that truly

has passed the test of time.

Your example keeps hope alive.

The key is no key! Like these two, neither

Will allow the music to end!

An example of sustainable love!

Narrative for "About Happiness"

A poem about "Happiness"

About Happiness

Am I who I think I am?

Could I be as perfect as I sometimes think

Or, am I in reality the failure I believe is me.

**** **** **** **** **** **** ****

I believe I am happy and most of the time I smile.

But of what value is my happiness if those around me are not. How can I make it contagious? Why can't they see that happiness is of the most importance in our lives.

I believe my goal in life is to be happy and to share that happiness with someone I love.

I think those who are happy try to remain that way.

Those who are unhappy, are trying to find happiness

And those who have never known happiness don't now what void there is in their life.

Some may think happiness is too much to expect of life. Others, that happiness simply does not exist. Still others will only associate happiness with a time long ago.

Many people may feel they don't deserve to be happy. And I believe there are those who enjoy being unhappy!

Narrative for Anticipation

This very short poem expresses what we all experience!

Anticipation

Holding to the highest expectations

You shoulder the repeated disappointment.

Now accepting the wait, your expectations shift

a little

This period can be torment

Your anticipation you hate

Serendipity

The occurrence and development

Of events by chance in a happy

And beneficial way

(Stroke of serendipity)

Narrative for "In These Times"

Society today has become horribly

compromised.

Government flip flop on doctrine.

Senseless murder is committed in schools,

houses and any place people gather.

Certainly this appears to be the "End of Times".

My poem addresses this condition.

In These Times

This is one of those times

One of those times when

Your faith is all that you have

All that represents some hope

If that faith is your

Last level of defense and nothing

Can penetrate that.

Then! How blessed you are.

Narrative for She Knew

This poem is a response to "He Knows" in "The Reluctant Poet" the first in the series!!

She Knew

The young girls wonder what the future holds

Family, children things like that

While their counterpart, the young lads, frolic

At this point she does not know?

A mother, wife? She wonders about this life?

As the girl reaches "Womanhood"

The boys they start to notice.

Wow!! Who Knew?

She Knew!!

Her skirt gets shorter,

Her legs ger longer!

The fellas now begin the chase…

She knew!!

www.ingramcontent.com/pod-product-compliance
Lightning Source LLC
Chambersburg PA
CBHW060608030426
42337CB00019B/3662